8/1

**THREE RIVERS
PUBLIC LIBRARY**
www.three-rivers-library.org
MINOOKA BRANCH LIBRARY
MINOOKA, IL 60447
815-467-1600

This book has been published in cooperation with Evans Publishing Group.

© Evans Brothers Limited 2010
This edition published under license from Evans Brothers Limited.

Published in the United States by
Amicus
P.O. Box 1329, Mankato, Minnesota 56002

Printed in China by New Era Printing Co.Ltd

Library of Congress Cataloging-in-Publication Data

Ensaff, Najoud.
  Retail careers / by Najoud Ensaff and Anne Rooney.
    p. cm. -- (In the workplace)
  Includes bibliographical references and index.
  Summary: "Describes jobs in the retail industry. Includes information on retail managers,
customer service, buyers, supply chain managers, warehouse managers, and more, covering
their responsibilities and training needed. Also includes profiles of workers in the industry"--Provided by publisher.
  ISBN 978-1-60753-093-0 (library binding)
  1. Retail trade--Vocational guidance--Juvenile literature. 2. Selling--Vocational guidance--Juvenile literature. I. Rooney,
Anne. II. Title.
  HF5429.29.E57 2011
  381'.1023--dc22

                                                                    2009054195

Editor and picture researcher: Patience Coster
Designer: Guy Callaby

We are grateful to the following for permission to reproduce photographs: Alamy 6 (Interfoto), 7 (John Norman), 10
(Malcolm Case-Green), 14 (Justin Kase zninez), 21 (Kevin Foy), 24 (Blend Images), 25 (Peter Treanor), 32 (Ian Shaw),
34 (CountryCollection – Homer Sykes), 38 (Keith Morris), 41 (Alex Segre), 42 (Caro); Corbis 8 (Gideon Mendel), 9
(Gideon Mendel), 11 (Peter Dench), 12 (Creasource), 13 (Dex Images, Inc.), 15 (Satchan), 16 (Alex Hofford/epa), 17
(Richard Baker), 18 (Atlantide Phototravel), 19 (Aaron Black), 20 (Benoit Tessier/Reuters), 22 (Ulrich Perrey/dpa), 26
(Richard Baker), 27 (Andrew Lichtenstein), 29 (Edward Bock), 31 (Don Mason), 33 (Justin Lane/epa), 37 (Sven
Hagolani), 43 (Atlantide Phototravel); Getty Images 23 (Zigy Kaluzny), 28 (VEER Mark Adams), 30 (Jetta
Productions), 36 (Seth Joel), 39 (AFP), 40 (Gary Burchell); Shutterstock cover (Marco_Sc).

05 10
PO1568

9 8 7 6 5 4 3 2 1

IN THE
WORKPLACE

Retail Careers

NAJOUD ENSAFF
AND **ANNE ROONEY**

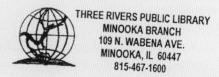

amicus
mankato, minnesota

Contents

The World of Retail

Retail—selling goods to customers—is a huge and vibrant industry. In the United States, 15.3 million people worked in retail in 2008. They work in big and small businesses, ranging from independent shops and boutiques, to supermarkets and large retail stores, to superstores and giant international chains. Not all retail outlets are shops—online retailers, shopping catalogs, and auctioneers are all in the retail business. Within these different settings there are many roles and opportunities demanding a wide variety of skills and personalities.

TO WORK IN RETAIL, YOU WILL NEED

●

to work well in a team

●

to have an interest in selling and merchandise

●

to enjoy working with people

●

to be customer focused

RETAIL—IT'S NOT JUST SELLING

The public face of retail is the sales assistants and management staff you see in stores when you go shopping, but there is far more to the world of retail. If you enjoy working with people, you might like to deal directly with customers on the storeroom floor or work in human resources. If you like to work with numbers,

Department stores such as Macy's in New York City employ a vast number of people in retail jobs, including managers, buyers, and sales assistants.

you could choose the financial side of retail, or managing and controlling stock (goods to sell). If you like design and have a good "eye," you might create window displays or design the web site of an online store. Or you might like to work in buying, choosing new products to sell. Whichever area you decide to make your career in, you will be aiming—with the rest of the team you work with—toward increasing sales and profit for your organization.

Retail outlets include independent shops, such as this bakery in Jerusalem, Israel. Employees of smaller operations may be promoted quickly, but they need to have a mature and responsible attitude toward their work.

GOODS FOR SALE

Retail is all about selling. If you choose to work in retail, you might sell fresh food or designer fashion, e-books or cars, or anything in between. You will need to be passionate about the products you work with—you must really believe they are the best if you are to persuade people to buy them. Choosing the area of retail you want to work in is as important as deciding on the role you want.

SUIT YOURSELF

When choosing a job and retail sector, you need to think about your own personality, interests, and strengths. Are you good at looking at an overall plan, at analyzing a problem, or at dealing face to face with people? Are you good with numbers? Do you have an eye for detail? Are you creative, with lots of ideas? Are you a well-organized person? Do you like to travel? Are you happy working shifts? Knowing what skills you have will help you to find an area and a role that suits you.

FINDING A JOB
Jobs in retail are advertised online and in trade magazines and newspapers. When you are starting out, perhaps looking for a weekend or seasonal job, the easiest way to find a position is to look for vacancies advertised in store windows or go into a store you like and ask.

On the Shop Floor

The most obvious aspect of retail is selling to the public in a store. This is an environment we are all familiar with from our everyday lives, and most people don't give much thought to what is involved in it. The work carried out in stores or other retail outlets is called "store operations."

RETAIL MANAGER

Every store has a manager who is responsible for its day-to-day running. In a large organization with more than one store, there is a management chain, up to the head office. The manager of a large store will have help from assistants and managers of different departments or floors. In a smaller shop, the manager will personally take on a wider range of tasks and responsibilities.

A store manager is responsible for the smooth running of the store. He or she must make sure that there is enough stock of the right type properly displayed, that there are trained staff on hand, that the premises open on time and are clean, well-run, and welcoming to customers, and that the store meets its targets and is profitable.

Managers of large supermarkets must ensure that communication between different areas is effective and that customers are treated well.

MAIN TASKS: STORE MANAGER

●

ensuring the store is attractive and that staff give customers good service

●

monitoring staff progress

●

checking stock and staffing levels

●

deciding on and meeting sales targets

●

working with senior managers

●

ensuring health and safety regulations are met

Store managers are responsible for making sure that high standards of health and sanitation are maintained.

MANAGING PEOPLE

Managers may be responsible for recruiting and training staff, for organizing work schedules and shifts, and for handling any disciplinary matters relating to staff. They are involved in setting targets for their staff and monitoring their progress. Motivating staff and dealing with their problems can be a particularly rewarding part of working with people. In a large organization, a human resources department will help with recruiting, training, and disciplining staff, but day-to-day staff management is still the responsibility of the store manager.

BUSINESS MANAGEMENT

A manager must set targets for the business and make sure they are achieved. This usually means setting and meeting sales figures. To achieve targets, the manager must make the store and its stock attractive to customers so that they come in and spend money. In many cases, the manager oversees selecting and buying stock, and advertising or promoting the store.

HANDY HINT
You are more likely to win a place on a management training program if you can gain some experience in a retail environment. There are often temporary or part-time jobs available in stores and restaurants, which you can do while you are still in high school or college. This will help you to choose the area of retail that most interests you, and it will show employers that you have made an informed choice and have genuine enthusiasm.

LIFE AS A RETAIL MANAGER

Managers usually spend some time each day walking the shop floor, checking the displays and stock, and making sure customers are well served. The manager also has overall responsibility for health and safety, and for making sure the business is run legally. This requires knowledge of the law and of financial practices.

Managers in small stores usually have a more hands-on role and more independence than those in chain stores such as Walmart or Macy's. In a large retail chain, functions such as recruitment, stock selection, and promotion are carried out by staff at the company headquarters.

Store managers in a retail chain are in close contact with senior managers at its headquarters or regional office, and they need to make sure their store is run and develops in line with national strategies.

Managers of grocery stores must monitor stock supplies and instruct staff to make certain that food does not pass its expiration date.

**TO WORK AS
A RETAIL MANAGER,
YOU WILL NEED**
●
*strong leadership and
organizational skills*
●
good communication skills
●
*the ability to prioritize and
delegate work*
●
*the ability to work well
under pressure*

DEPARTMENT MANAGER

Department managers are responsibile for a department or area of the store, such as household appliances or the checkouts in a supermarket. The department manager looks after staff, stock, and equipment in his or her area, making staff work schedules, organizing restocking of shelves, making sure checkouts are staffed, and that the area is neat, clean, and attractive.

The department manager spends much of the day on the shop floor making sure that everything is running smoothly. Department managers often have direct contact with customers, answering questions, dealing with problems, and making recommendations. You will need good "people skills" to be a department manager: the ability to listen sympathetically, to be polite to distressed or angry customers, and to offer constructive solutions to problems. You may also have to deal with difficult situations such as shoplifting or breakages by customers, lost children, and people becoming sick or having an accident in the store.

Kevin: Department Manager

"I joined this supermarket chain when I left school, working on the checkouts. It's a large chain, so there are lots of opportunities for in-store training. I showed I was a good worker, so I quickly got on to a fast-track training program. I became first a team leader and then a [department] manager. I've just completed a degree while keeping my full-time job. Some people come into [management after earning a degree], but I wanted to get straight to work and further my education while earning.

"My day-to-day work involves managing the staff working on the checkouts and taking care of all health and safety and customer care issues relating to the checkouts. I organize work schedules, I decide when to put out a call for more staff, and I'm the one who has to cope if the technology breaks down. There's never a dull day, and I'm working on progressing my management career at the same time."

Among other things, department managers need to deal with problems that arise, such as customer complaints and supply shortages.

PERSONAL SHOPPER

Some stores employ personal shoppers, who work with individual customers to meet their needs. A personal shopper advises people on their purchases. He or she might help them choose an outfit for a particular occasion, or renew their wardrobe for a new season or a change in their life. Personal shoppers often work in fashion departments, but some stores offer the service in home furnishings and other areas.

FASHION KNOW-HOW

Personal shoppers need to combine good judgment in color and fashion with tact and sensitivity toward their clients.

To be a personal shopper working in fashion, you will need to understand how colors and fabrics work together, know about trends in clothing and fashions, and understand how different styles, cuts, and colors suit different body shapes and complexions. You will need a good eye for design and detail.

You will work with people of different ages and shapes, some with quite specific requirements and others who do not really know what they want and who will rely heavily on your advice. You will need to read fashion magazines and follow fashion closely as some—though not all—clients will want to follow current trends. You will need to be a good judge of character and be able to understand customers' taste in order to suggest items they will like.

TO WORK AS A PERSONAL SHOPPER, YOU WILL NEED

•

a good knowledge of fashion

•

an understanding of how colors and fabrics work together and of which styles suit which body types

•

good interpersonal and communication skills

WHO PAYS?

Personal shoppers who work for a large store are paid by the store. The service may be offered free to shoppers, or they may pay a fee to be kept up to date with new lines or products. If you work in-house in a store, you will need to know the product range of the store very well. You will be recommending items from the store's full range, and you will need to be able to put together outfits using items and accessories from different departments.

Some personal shoppers work freelance and choose items from a number of different stores. In this case, the customer pays a fee directly to the personal shopper. Some people prefer to use freelance personal shoppers as their advice is impartial—they are not bound to recommend items from one store, but can pick from any number of outlets.

There is a growing number of online personal shoppers who source items for customers from online stores. They carry out product research and price comparison on any type of goods, then advise the customer of the best buys. This is usually a freelance career.

Personal shoppers who work in-house must be very knowledgeable about the store's merchandise and able to describe it in a clear and appealing way.

HANDY HINT
As with anyone working freelance, personal shoppers have to keep track of their income and spending so that they can do their accounting correctly and work within the law.

CUSTOMER SERVICE REPRESENTATIVE

The customer service department in a retail organization deals with questions and complaints. Sometimes customers will be upset or angry, so it takes tact and patience to work successfully in customer service. The manager of a customer service desk or department will often be called in to give a final decision on problems, or to solve particular problems that are not covered by company guidelines. The customer service representative has responsibility for the safety of staff, making sure they are not attacked or abused by angry customers.

GETTING IT RIGHT

The public image of a company often relies on how well the customer service department deals with problems. Customers who are not satisfied with their treatment may complain to customer protection organizations or the media, or publicly post their frustrations on the Internet. This can be very damaging to the organization, but it can be avoided by good customer relations staff.

You may be involved in developing customer service policy in discussions with management and legal advisers. You will need to implement any new policies and train staff in new procedures, as well as monitor the performance of the department and check customer satisfaction.

Customer service representatives need to be good listeners and to have people skills so that they can respond effectively to customer inquiries and complaints.

TO WORK AS A CUSTOMER SERVICE REPRESENTATIVE, YOU WILL NEED

●

good communication skills

●

to be diplomatic and patient

●

the ability to remain polite when dealing with customers who are upset or angry

IS THE CUSTOMER ALWAYS RIGHT?

Customers are protected by consumer protection laws that state that anything they buy must be safe, must be fit for its intended purpose, and must work properly. In addition, many retail organizations offer extra guarantees or extended warranties on goods, or allow customers to exchange things if they change their mind about a purchase. If you work as a customer service manager, you will need to know the law about consumer purchases and your organization's policy on exchanges and faulty goods.

You will need a good knowledge of the product range —sometimes people will think an item is faulty when they are actually using it incorrectly. Occasionally, customers may claim something was faulty when they bought it, but it is clear that they have broken it. Dealing with tricky situations like this while remaining polite is a challenging and rewarding part of customer service.

In a store, members of the customer service team work with customers face-to-face, but in other retail organizations, customer support may be carried out over the phone or by e-mail.

MAIN TASKS: CUSTOMER SERVICE MANAGER

●

running a customer service desk or department

●

giving help and advice to customers face-to-face, over the telephone, or by e-mail

●

investigating and solving customers' problems and complaints

●

issuing refunds, exchanges, or compensation

●

arranging services for customers

●

developing feedback and complaints procedures

●

recruiting and training staff

If a customer wants to exchange an item, staff need to be polite and helpful.

Buying and Selling

All retail businesses work by buying stock and selling it on to customers at a higher price. Two very important aspects of this process are ordering the right stock in the first place and persuading people to buy it.

RETAIL BUYER

If a store is to succeed, it needs to stock goods that customers want to buy. It is the job of a buyer to find just the right items. Buyers usually specialize in a particular type of product, such as toys, fashion accessories, electrical goods, books, or music. They build up expertise in their field and develop detailed knowledge of the market, including all the suppliers, the various methods of manufacturing, and the different areas of the market. For example, someone who specializes in buying luggage will need to know the difference between luxury products and value ranges, how luggage made from leather and luggage made from man-made materials differs, and which will suit the customers of a particular store.

TO BECOME A BUYER, YOU WILL NEED

●

a strong commercial awareness

●

an understanding of what motivates customers to buy products

●

good analytical skills

●

creativity and the ability to predict future trends

A retail buyer and a seller negotiate terms at a trade fair in China.

A buyer assesses a range of menswear in advance of a fashion show in London.

FINDING THE BEST—WHEREVER IT MAY BE

Buyers often have to travel to visit suppliers, trade fairs, and shows where they can see new products coming on to the market, compare prices and quality, and choose which items to buy. They may need to go to the factories where goods are made to check standards. It is not just a matter of making sure the product is good enough. Many retailers today have responded to public pressure to make sure that their goods are ethically sourced and produced. Buyers may need to check that workers in a garment factory or on a farm are fairly treated and work in a safe environment, as this may be a condition of the store's contract with the supplier.

A buyer may work in a store or from the headquarters of a retail chain. Working in a store, a buyer might have to schedule visits from prospective suppliers who want to show their product line in the hope of getting a contract. The buyer needs to know what customers will buy and the prices they will be prepared to pay. Buyers look at computerized records of sales to see what has sold well in the past and combine this with their experience of the market and new trends to decide which product lines the store should stock.

**MAIN TASKS:
RETAIL BUYER**
●
choosing products and lines
●
placing supplier orders and negotiating contracts
●
analyzing trends and consumer buying patterns
●
attending shows or trade fairs to find new products and suppliers
●
evaluating product quality
●
presenting collections to senior retail managers

SPECIAL KNOWLEDGE

Some areas require special knowledge and also change rapidly. Fashion buyers, for instance, go to fashion shows and watch developing trends so that they can judge what will be popular in coming months. Other areas that require special knowledge include wine, antiques, cars, motorcycles, and consumer electronics. In fields like these, it is important to have a genuine interest in the product range.

In a small store, the buyer may need to deal with a range of different types of products, or with all the products the store stocks.

CHANGING MARKETS

A buyer needs to be able to keep up with trends in consumer purchasing and predict the direction in which trends are likely to go. Buyers also need to notice and respond quickly to changes in spending patterns among shoppers.

Picking objects that are likely to be popular as Christmas presents, or the latest fashion in clothes, takes practice and a real feel for the market. When a buyer gets it right, the store can make a large profit—but mistakes can be very expensive, so it's a big responsibility. Buyers choose stock many months ahead of it being in the store, so they are always thinking a couple of seasons ahead, choosing Christmas items in summer, for example.

Two women are drawn to the clothes on display in a shop window in Milan, Italy. The success or failure of a store depends on the choices made by retail buyers.

Kairi: Retail Buyer

"I work as the buyer for a small chain of gift shops in airports. Many of our products have a patriotic theme, and some of it is perishable—food such as smoked salmon and [candy]. I choose all the items that are stocked in our outlets. Some of them come from very small suppliers—craftsmen and women working on their own or in a small cooperative—while others are produced by huge manufacturers. I have to negotiate prices, keep track of stock, and analyze sales figures so that I know what is selling and what is not—there's no point in [ordering] more of something that is very hard to [sell].

A buyer examines teapots. It is vital that buyers have an instinct for items that will sell.

"Some of the items we sell are made to our own designs. I find this aspect of the job most exciting, as I work with designers and producers to make something that is unique. These specialty products are based on what I believe will sell, from my knowledge of the market and analysis of our sales figures. I have to find suppliers and work closely with them through all stages of the process.

"Generally, I have a good relationship with suppliers we use a lot, so I enjoy visiting them and showing them around our stores when they come to see how the merchandise is displayed. I feel I've something to be proud of in a well-stocked outlet that sees a lot of customer [traffic]."

WINDOW DRESSER

A window dresser makes attractive displays of stock in a window, with the aim of making the store appeal to passing customers so that they go inside. Window dressers might have to put together special themed displays (for Christmas, for instance) or promote a particular range or type of stock. Clothing stores and department stores often put a lot of effort into building attractive window displays and changing them frequently. Window dressing is part of visual merchandising, the field that covers all aspects of displaying goods and making a store attractive and easy for customers to navigate.

A dresser arranges motorized puppets in the window of a Paris department store.

TO BECOME A WINDOW DRESSER, YOU WILL NEED

●

an eye for color and for textures and shapes that go well together

●

retail experience

●

imagination and enthusiasm

●

physical fitness—you'll be moving things around and spending all day on your feet

FINDING A JOB

Most people start with a job in retail and then move into window dressing. Training in interior design is a good starting point, too. Most window dressers learn on the job and move into the work when they are already employed by a store.

Andrew: Window Dresser

"I work as a window dresser in a large department store in central London. It's a creative job—you need enthusiasm and flair. We have more than 300 feet (100 m) of windows and change the displays every few weeks. Changing a display takes two full days—one to move the old display out and clean the windows, then another to build the new display. There is also time in between spent working on the design and sourcing the items from around the store. The theme is set by management, but within that I have quite a lot of freedom to brief my team. I work out the designs, and some other members of the team do most of the arranging and picking items to include. I do a bit of that, too, as it helps me keep up-to-date with what's in the store.

"As well as the main window displays, we do little displays inside the store. These are important to customers, as they act as signposts to different departments—they can see a display from the escalator and think, 'Ah yes, there are the shoes . . . ' and head off in the right direction.

A jungle-themed Christmas window display in a department store in New York City.

"I work Monday to Friday, as Saturday is too busy to be standing on ladders making displays, and the shop has to look its best then. Some stores do it differently, and only change displays when the shop is closed.

"I love the job—there's always something new to do. The best thing is seeing customers outside gawking at a new display and pointing out to each other the parts they like best. That really raises my spirits."

PUBLIC RELATIONS MANAGER

Public relations (PR) is part of marketing a business or product. Working in PR involves helping to create, maintain, and promote a company's public image and profile. As a PR manager, you will think of ways to publicize the retail organization. You might also be involved in organizing events to bring more customers into the store, such as product launches, openings of new stores, book signings, visits from celebrities, and so on. You may have to pitch stories to journalists and organize advertising.

A POSITIVE IMAGE

People working in PR help to keep a retailer's brand name in the public eye. Jobs involve working with the media, writing press releases, and organizing publicity campaigns. PR involves using new media to reach the retailer's target audience. This can include podcasts, web sites, social networking sites, and company blogs, so you will need to keep up-to-date with current trends in technology. If you work in PR, you may need to speak in public, give radio or television interviews, and talk to the press. You may work alongside advertising agency staff to devise promotions, loyalty card programs, and other ways of boosting customers' interest in the store.

DEALING WITH TROUBLE

When there is a news story about a product, such as a question about product safety, it is the PR department that organizes the release of information to the media. It is important to balance customer safety and information with maintaining the store's good name.

TO BECOME A PR MANAGER, YOU WILL NEED

●

good time-management skills

●

confidence talking to journalists and others in the media

●

the ability to communicate effectively and persuasively in person and on paper

Public relations managers sometimes recruit famous names to help promote their products.

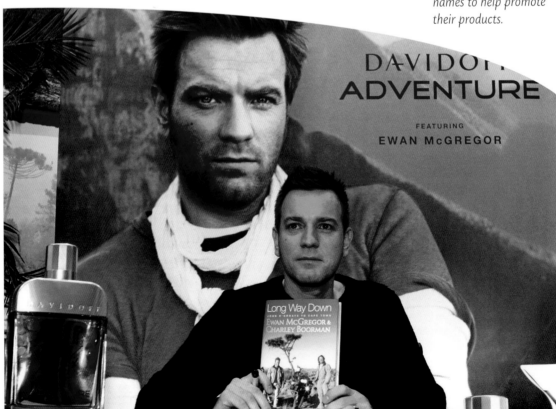

Tom: PR Manager

"I work for a mobile phone retailer, and my main responsibilities are to promote the company's image and communicate positively with the media. I got into PR after [college]. I chose to do a degree in public relations and, as part of my degree, I had to do [an internship] in a company. Luckily, they liked me and offered me a job after my degree, so I stayed on.

Public relations managers need to have excellent communication skills, both written and spoken. They must have the confidence to speak in public, when required.

"On a day-to-day basis, my job entails dealing with all the inquiries we receive. I also oversee the marketing of the chain of retail stores and its products through press releases and brochures. There's a lot of focus on deadlines, so being able to manage your time well is important in this job. I [work] with journalists who request information or interviews, and communicate directly with our PR agency. Usually I work between 9:00 a.m. and 5:30 p.m., but when we have big projects, I work longer hours. We're just working toward a set of promotions and a brochure, so things will get busy as the launch date nears.

"I enjoy my job because of the interaction I have with people. It can get really busy sometimes, especially when we're working on tight deadlines, but I find this stimulating."

The Supply Chain

Getting goods into the shops is a large part of retailing, though it's one people don't usually think about when it runs smoothly. The supply chain is the sequence of steps, people, and businesses involved in moving goods from producers to stores.

SUPPLY CHAIN MANAGER

A supply chain manager is responsible for making sure the process of supplying goods to stores runs smoothly. The job can involve sourcing and purchasing goods, together with logistics, transportation, warehousing and storage, and distribution (sending goods out to stores).

THE RIGHT THINGS IN THE RIGHT PLACE AT THE RIGHT TIME

Often, a retail chain orders stock from a wholesaler (a business that supplies in bulk), although some large chains deal directly with manufacturers or farmers. A large order of stock is moved—or shipped—to the retailer's warehouse, then sent out to shops when it is needed. It is important to judge the stock level to hold in the warehouse and in stores correctly. Keeping unsold stock ties up space and money and reduces profit, but running out of popular items can also be an expensive mistake.

Some organizations run a "just in time" stock system, which means they order stock just in time to send it out again. This system depends on precise timing and good judgment so that shops do not run out of vital stock. High-quality information about customers' buying patterns and sophisticated computerized stock control systems make this possible.

MAIN TASKS: SUPPLY CHAIN MANAGER

●

setting and monitoring levels of stock

●

managing the shipment of goods

●

making sure targets are met

●

logistics

●

warehouse management

●

improving supply networks

Supply chain managers keep computerized records of the huge quantities of stock in their warehouse.

Supply chain managers decide on the best methods of transportation for their products.

SUPPLY AND DEMAND

The demand for many goods changes with the seasons, the weather, or the state of the economy. The supply chain manager has to assess demand ahead of time, and this is not always easy. When there is a wet, cold summer, for instance, many shops are left with stock of grills and other hot-weather items. A surprise Christmas hit can leave shops sold out of a popular item, thus losing sales. In fashion and fresh foods, correctly judging stock levels is important all the time.

LOGISTICS

Logistics involves figuring out how to get goods from one place to another and managing their flow. Logistics are often handled by a supply chain manager, though some organizations have separate logistics managers. The work involves using computers and working with many other people. If you work in this area, you may have to decide on methods of transportation (air, sea, rail, or road) and manage the stocking and layout of warehouses to make the movement of goods in and out as efficient as possible.

FINDING A JOB
A degree in logistics, transportation management, geography, international transportation, or supply chain management will give you a good start. Large stores may require a bachelor's or even a master's degree in this area. All will require on-the-job training in the specifics of their business.

At this supermarket warehouse, goods are loaded directly onto trucks by way of conveyor belts.

WAREHOUSE AND STOCK MANAGER

After goods have been bought from a producer or wholesaler, they are stored in a warehouse until they have to be sent out to a store. Warehousing is an important stage in retailing. The warehouse and inventory must be properly managed so that stores can be supplied promptly.

In larger organizations, warehouse management and inventory control are separate tasks, but in smaller organizations, the warehouse manager may also carry out inventory control.

MANAGING A WAREHOUSE

The warehouse manager is responsible for the day-to-day running of the warehouse, safe storage of inventory, and maintenance of all vehicles, machinery, and equipment. It is the manager's job to plan requirements for storage and equipment and make sure all inventory is properly and securely handled and stored. The manager must make sure all staff are trained and follow health and safety guidelines in their work, as a warehouse can be a dangerous environment in which to work.

TO BECOME A WAREHOUSE AND STOCK MANAGER, YOU WILL NEED

●

good management skills

●

physical fitness

●

an understanding of the inventory and its transportation and storage requirements

●

knowledge of health and safety issues and practices

Most warehouses use automated and computerized systems. If you work as a warehouse manager, you will need to be confident with these systems, as you will have to produce reports and statistical charts for headquarters.

The warehousing of perishable items such as fresh food is particularly challenging. The warehouse manager must make sure the temperature and humidity levels are correct, and that the oldest stock leaves the warehouse first so that none has a chance to deteriorate or spoil.

INVENTORY CONTROL

Stock control involves controlling the flow of products into and out of the warehouse. Inventory control involves checking incoming shipments of goods, organizing their storage, and having them moved to the right place in the warehouse. Products must be properly labeled and stored so that they can be found easily. Most stock controllers use handheld scanners to read barcodes on goods moving in and out of the warehouse and between locations. The computerized inventory system is automatically updated with stock levels and locations. When the register in a store reads a barcode on an item, the inventory control system is updated. In this way, the store and the warehouse communicate so that sold goods can be quickly replaced.

MAIN TASKS: WAREHOUSE AND STOCK MANAGER

●

managing staff who work in the warehouse

●

planning and securing storage

●

supplying and maintaining equipment and vehicles

●

managing the premises, ensuring security and correct storage conditions

●

organizing staff training

●

tracking and managing stock movement

●

producing reports and working with headquarters

●

dealing with suppliers and hauling companies

In such a vast space as a warehouse, stock control and monitoring is all-important.

Behind the Scenes

There are many jobs behind the scenes in a store or other retail outlet. You might not give any thought to these when you go shopping yourself, but if you are thinking about a career in retail, you will find that plenty of interesting opportunities are not on the shoproom floor. Some of these are jobs that exist in many sectors and involve transferable skills, but you may choose to work at them in retail because it is a lively, vibrant environment.

HUMAN RESOURCES MANAGER

The human resources (HR) team deals with recruiting, developing, and retaining staff. It helps managers by advising them on human resources policies and putting systems in place to help managers develop their own staff.

HR managers are responsible for all aspects of staffing. They monitor absences, manage risks, and organize staff training and development. They are often involved in recruiting new staff, or overseeing the recruitment officers who do this. HR managers need to be familiar with employment law and company policies and procedures. They may need to visit departments within the company and get to know the staffing issues they face. If you are considering this as a career, you need to develop good people skills and analytical abilities.

Human resources managers need to ensure that companies employ the right balance of staff in terms of skills and experience.

An important part of a human resources manager's job is to interview and select employees.

FINDING A JOB
Many retailers offer employees entry into human resources roles with on-the-job training. Many colleges also offer degrees in human resources management, and an internship that gives you work experience plus college credit can be a good way to get your foot in the door.

TO BECOME A HUMAN RESOURCES MANAGER, YOU WILL NEED
- *knowledge of employment law*
- *good communication skills*
- *problem-solving abilities*
- *analytical and people skills*

SOLVING PROBLEMS
An important part of the human resources manager's job is dealing with any disputes and disciplinary matters. Sometimes these relate to sensitive issues such as discrimination, sexual harassment, or bullying, so the HR manager needs to be tactful and sensitive.

RECRUITMENT
Recruitment involves finding the right person with the appropriate skills and qualifications to fill each job. The needs of a company must be matched with the skills of a job seeker. A recruitment officer needs to be a good judge of character and have a good understanding of the structure, culture, and ethos of the organization. Anyone working in recruitment must be able to pick staff with not only the right qualifications and experience, but also the qualities to do the job well and fit in with the organization and other staff. It is important to know and follow equal opportunity laws and policies when recruiting staff.

WORKING WITH PEOPLE
Once staff are in place, their professional development is the responsibility of the HR manager. Staff training and assessment, review meetings, incentive programs, and motivation are all handled by the HR manager and his or her team. When members of the staff leave, the HR manager usually interviews them to find out why. The results of these interviews can help the organization to improve conditions and retain future staff.

INFORMATION TECHNOLOGY SPECIALIST

Like many sectors, retail depends increasingly on computer technology to run smoothly. Computers are used to operate payroll and other aspects of finance, to produce all kinds of documents and presentations, to run stock control systems linked to computerized tills, and in many other areas. Tills, barcode scanners, and even the equipment that controls the temperature and humidity are all computerized. If you want to work in IT, there are many opportunities within retail to put your skills to good use.

WEB DESIGN

Most retailers have a web site, and for online retailers such as Amazon, it is the core of their business. Working on a retailer's web site can involve the use of design and graphics, producing animation or Flash movies, adding sound and videos, or working on large, complex databases and e-commerce systems.

KEEPING THINGS GOING

Large computer networks need a comprehensive systems support team to keep them running properly. If you work in systems support, you could be installing hardware (new terminals, for example), installing or writing software, training users or giving them technical support, or designing or sourcing new software or hardware. You may need to work odd hours, and you may need to travel between sites.

TO WORK IN IT, YOU WILL NEED

- *good technical skills*

- *experience with a range of hardware and software*

- *communication skills, as you will need to deal with non-technical staff and explain complex matters to them*

Companies with complex computer networks will have a team of IT experts to maintain and update the system.

FINANCE SPECIALIST

A career in retail finance will mean you are helping the organization to find money to run, develop its business, and plan for the future. You may be involved in analyzing financial figures, measuring performance, and making strategic recommendations. You might analyze the success of a product promotion or look at how well certain stores are performing. There are many departments that need people trained in finance, including purchasing, payroll, and accounting.

TO WORK IN FINANCE, YOU WILL NEED

●

to be good with figures

●

a clear understanding of how business operates

●

the ability to explain technical information clearly

●

good analytical skills

Souad: Business Development Analyst

"I studied business [in college], specializing in finance in my last year. During [an internship], I worked in retail, in store management, and after graduation I worked for the same company for a year. I gained some great experience related to shop refitting and staff issues, but I wasn't using my financial skills, and I wanted to. As I lived near an Asda superstore, and the company had a good reputation, it seemed the obvious choice.

"I applied to Asda's graduate program, picking a financial route. I am now a business development analyst supporting the promotional and pricing team.

"I enjoy working for a big company. It's allowed me to use my financial skills and has provided me with a good career path and many financial benefits—I've even become a Walmart shareholder."

A business development analyst needs to be able to explain financial strategies in a clear and concise way.

Not Just Stores

Not all retail takes place in shop premises. Other types of retailers include auction houses, online retailers, catalog and mail-order retailers, and telephone call centers.

AUCTIONEER

An auctioneer runs an auction at which items are sold to the person who is prepared to pay the most—the person who makes the highest bid. The auctioneer shows and describes each item and invites prospective buyers to make a bid, which means suggesting a price they are prepared to pay. Bidders compete against one another, offering more money each time, dropping out as they reach the most they are willing to pay. When only one buyer is left, that person has won the auction and pays the last price he or she bid. The auction house takes a percentage of the price paid to cover its own costs and pay the auctioneer, and the seller takes the rest of the money. Some auctioneers buy up stock and then auction it, taking all the profit, as they have already paid for the goods.

The famous auction houses such as Christie's and Sotheby's are international organizations that deal in all types of fine art objects and antiques. But there are many smaller, local auction houses that sell everything from bric-a-brac to cars, houses, antiques, wine, and farm animals.

Buyers crowd in for an auction of Impressionist art in London.

Sotheby's	
Lot Number: 163	
USD ($)	6,000
EUR (€)	4,447
UK (£)	3,037
SWI (F)	7,361
RUB (R)	155,028
JPY (¥)	727,260

SPECIALIZED KNOWLEDGE

An auctioneer needs a very good knowledge of the type of stock he or she deals in. If you want to work for one of the big art auction houses, you will need a degree in art history; if you want to work at a car auction, you will need a detailed knowledge of cars. To work in property auctions, you would need good knowledge of houses and may have worked as a real estate agent.

As well as recognizing the qualities of an object and describing it appropriately, the auctioneer needs to know the approximate value of the item in order to manage the bidding. It takes a good memory to remember small details about many different items, yet it's recognizing some tiny feature that often helps an auctioneer identify an object. Many people bring items they have inherited to auction houses. They often don't know anything about the object or where it came from, and they need the auctioneer to tell them what it is worth and a bit of its history.

Auctioneers need particular knowledge of the stock they are selling. This auctioneer is leading the bidding in a sale of African, Oceanic, and Pre-Columbian art.

TO WORK AS AN AUCTIONEER, YOU WILL NEED

confidence—this is a role carried out in public

good presentation and communication skills

detailed knowledge of the items you work with

a good memory

FIND A JOB

Many auction houses offer internships. These require you to work in the auction house without pay for a few weeks, but during that time you will learn the ropes. You will carry out some very basic tasks, but you will see in detail how the auction process works.

Neil: Auctioneer

"I deal in antique toys. I identify them and describe them in a catalog that is sent out to a list of clients and available to anyone else who might want to buy. I work with regular suppliers, but I also pick things up at fairs and charity shops. We put the items on display a week before the sale so that people can see them and ask any questions.

"The auction itself gives me a real buzz. The room is crowded; there are phone lines for phone bidders and a video link for online bidders. It's a performance—you have to get people to relax and get them into the rhythm of the sale. And it's important not to talk so quickly that people don't understand what you're saying. Some people come from abroad to buy, so English is not their first language. Speaking slowly and clearly helps them.

"In the lead-up to a sale, I often have to research the items I'm selling—find out where they were made, how old they are, what they're worth, who might have used them . . . This information goes into the catalog. And then sometimes a buyer will ask another question, and I'll have to do more research. It's rewarding and challenging—it can turn into a bit of detective work sometimes.

This auctioneer is conducting a sale of items from a country house. He will be educated in a relevant subject, such as art history.

"It's very rewarding when someone comes along with something they suspect is a bit of old junk and it turns out to be really valuable or important. They don't always go on to sell it. Some people decide to keep an item that has a bit of a history."

SALES EXECUTIVE FOR AN ONLINE RETAILER

Online shopping is a growing sector of retail. In some areas, online sales are now a significant part of the market. The biggest difference for people working in online retail is that they do not come into direct contact with customers, and the web site takes the place of the store.

A sales executive for an online retailer may explore new and innovative ways of reaching customers and recruiting business partners to work with the retailer. Online retailers and suppliers can work closely together without the movement of physical store—the retailer provides a "storefront" for goods, and when a customer orders them, the supplier ships them. Many online retailers also have warehouses of stock, but electronic communication replaces stock movement increasingly.

Some products sold in online stores do not exist as physical objects. The role of a sales executive working with virtual products such as music, video, or software delivered by download is very different from that of someone working in sales in a real shop. Even so, the principles of marketing and sales, the financial transactions involved, and the customer psychology are much the same. A sales executive working in online retail needs an expert knowledge of the product range and customers' requirements, just as he or she would in a traditional retail environment.

TO WORK AS AN ONLINE SALES EXECUTIVE, YOU WILL NEED

- *excellent computer skills*
- *an innovative approach*
- *experience in sales or retail*

Sales executives working for online retailers such as Amazon can quickly build up profiles of customer buying patterns.

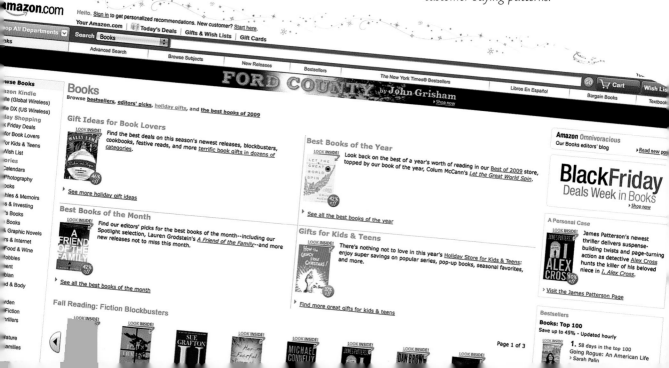

CALL CENTER MANAGER

Call center staff work with telephones to offer customer support or sell to customers. Customer support call centers deal with customers' questions and problems. Often, selling from a call center is "cold calling"—phoning people who have not previously expressed an interest in a product or service. The call center manager is responsible for the staff, the equipment, and the smooth running of the call center.

KNOWING THE PRODUCT

Many call centers run help lines for electronic products such as computers and mobile phones. The staff—including the call center manager—need a very good understanding of the products they are supporting or selling and the types of problems customers may have with them. They need to be able to explain technical information to people who do not have any expert knowledge, and talk customers through instructions clearly and calmly in small steps. If you work as a call center manager, you will have to take over when a customer is not satisfied with or does not understand the support he or she gets from a call center worker, or when a call is too complicated for the member of staff who has taken the call.

**TO BE A
CALL CENTER MANAGER,
YOU WILL NEED**

●

*a good telephone manner and
communication skills*

●

tact and patience

●

management skills

●

*to be able to perform well
under pressure*

*Call center managers must
be able to cope well with
the demands of a
stressful environment.*

STAFF SUPPORT

The call center manager is responsible for training and motivating staff, setting targets for calls made or answered, and for monitoring staff progress and setting work schedules. In a large call center, there will be team leaders who provide first-line support to staff working the phone lines, and these team leaders will report to the call center manager.

Working in a call center can be stressful for staff, so the manager needs to provide strong support. Customers who are disappointed with a product or service or who feel their problems are not being dealt with sometimes get angry and aggressive. People who have been cold-called may be abusive and rude if they resent the intrusion of an unwanted phone call. It is difficult for staff to deal with this all day, and they need a supportive environment to help them cope.

The turnover of staff in call centers is often high, so the manager may spend a lot of time recruiting and training new staff. It is a challenging environment to work in and to manage. A good call center, though, can be very successful. Income is often related to the number of sales or calls processed, so the manager of a successful center can earn a lot.

Call center workers should have a polite and friendly telephone manner. They must remain calm even if their customers do not.

HANDY HINT
Some call centers are based abroad, so there may be the chance to work overseas. Some young people fund travel by working for a while in a call center in India or elsewhere. This type of experience can help you gain a position in a call center as a management trainee. Most call center managers begin as call center workers and work their way up.

On Your Own

A career in retail doesn't always mean working for a large organization. Some people work in small family shops, set up their own shop, or run a market stall. The Internet has provided a great opportunity for people to start their own retail businesses online, too.

ONLINE SELLER

It can be very expensive to set up a shop, but it costs very little to set up an online store. Many people who would love to have their own shop but can't raise the money or can't afford to give up their regular job set up online shops. There are many advantages: You don't have to work regular hours, you don't need to pay for premises and staff, and you can attract customers from around the world rather than rely on people who are physically nearby walking into your shop.

Many people who set up an online shop do so because they make their own products or have a passion for a particular type of product. Their stock may be a special interest with a market too spread out for a physical shop. Or they may run their online shop as a hobby or for extra income while studying or working at another job.

Small shopkeepers often rely on a combination of customer traffic and online sales.

Kathryn: Online Shopkeeper

"I have an online shop selling antique French fabrics. I am passionate about old fabrics, and I dreamed for years of having a little shop to sell them, but I live in a remote area of Wales, and I would have had to move—no one would find my shop here! Selling online is perfect for me. I have some regular customers in the United States and Canada, and I often sell to interior designers working on restoring old houses in France. I've sold quite a bit to people making films, too.

Searching for fabrics to sell online. The Internet is a perfect vehicle for owners of small businesses.

"I buy my fabrics in France. I go over for a couple of weeks at a time and tour the antique fairs, flea markets, old junk shops, and auctions. I collect vast quantities of fabric and bring it all back in my car. Some needs cleaning or restoring, and sometimes I have to [take apart] clothes or other items to reclaim the fabric. Then I photograph everything and write a description of it, including where it's from and its date. It's very different for customers buying fabric online, as they can't feel it, so I have to provide as much other information as possible.

"My prices are lower online than they would be if I had to rent a shop and employ staff. The price has to cover postage, of course, but that works out less than the other overheads would have been.

"Of course, I don't meet customers like I would in a real shop. But I've made online friendships with some of my regular customers, and I've learned what they like and are interested in. If I pick up something I know will be perfect for one of my customers, I e-mail them immediately and offer it before I put it in the shop. That's not something you can do in a real shop, and the customers really appreciate it. It's very rewarding—I'm working with a product I love and dealing with like-minded people who share my passion for it. I wouldn't change it for the world."

MARKET VENDOR

Several people who went on to build great business or retail empires started life selling things from a market stall. Traditional market stalls in farmers' markets, flea markets, and craft fairs sell anything from fruits and vegetables to craft items and cheap household goods. Some people choose to run a market stall because they make or grow their own products and want to sell them; others are excited by the challenge of buying goods cheaply and selling them quickly to make a profit. Running a market stall is hard physical work. You may need to move your stock to and from the stall every day, and you will have to open and close the stall, perhaps even building it and taking it apart each day. If your stall is outside, you will need stamina and good health, as you will be working in all weather.

Market vendors have more freedom than shop employees, but they need to be fit, as they are outdoors in all weather.

WHAT TO SELL?

If you want a market stall to sell something you grow or make yourself, you will need to make sure you have enough stock. You probably won't open your stall every day, as you will spend a lot of time collecting stock. But if you buy your stock—whether from farmers or wholesalers—you may be in your stall every day. Some products are seasonal, and you might need different suppliers to provide slightly different products over the year.

TO RUN A MARKET STALL, YOU WILL NEED

●

confidence

●

an outgoing personality

●

good health and physical fitness

BLUFF AND BLUSTER

The traditional image of a market vendor is of a loud, brash person who shouts to passersby, trying to get them to stop and look at the products. Most market vendors are not like this anymore, but they still need confidence and an outgoing personality.

You will need good interpersonal skills to work in a market stall, as you will be dealing with members of the public every day. You will also be working alongside other vendors and dealing with your suppliers. You will need the confidence to haggle, too—many people expect to negotiate prices with a market vendor. You will also need to negotiate prices with your suppliers.

An Italian fruit vendor. Market vendor work is often carried out by families and continued from one generation to the next.

HANDY HINT
You will need to do some careful research and calculations to set your prices so that you still make a profit but manage to attract enough customers. There might be some trial and error involved. If you sell all your stock very easily, you might be able to charge more; if sales are slow, you will do better to drop your prices and sell more.

INDEPENDENT SHOPKEEPER

You may choose to set up your own shop if you create a product or have a particular passion for some kind of product—or because you love the idea of having a shop. Running a shop is hard work, involving long hours. It can be high risk, as independent shops have to compete with big stores with a large workforce and more financing. When you start out, you will have to carry out all the tasks yourself, including organization, financing, administration, buying, marketing, and promotion, as well as stocking the shop and selling to customers.

RESEARCH

Researching products, competitors, suppliers, and prices before you start is vital. You will also need to decide where to set up your shop. Will it depend on passing customer traffic, or will people be prepared to go out of their way to find it? How will you promote it, letting people know it exists?

FINANCING

Setting up a shop is expensive. You may have savings or be able to borrow from your family, but many entrepreneurs take out a business loan from a bank. To do this, you will need to put together a business plan and estimate the cost—how much it will cost to rent premises, employ staff, buy stock, pay bills, and support yourself while your business gets going. Your research into products and suppliers and the viability of your business will feed into your business plan.

Independent shopkeeping is a risky business, but it can result in big financial rewards.

Getting to know your customers well is one of the most rewarding aspects of retail work.

WORKING ALONE

To work for yourself, you need to be motivated, be able to manage your time, and be willing to do any task. It can be very stressful as well as very exciting. Anyone working on their own needs to deal with their own accounts, including completing tax returns. You will need to keep all the receipts and other documents that you will need. You might want an accountant to help you with your accounts.

IS RETAIL RIGHT FOR YOU?

Retail is an exciting and lively sector of the economy. If you want to work in a vibrant environment, having contact with lots of people and dealing with a product range you love, retail can be very rewarding. There are so many roles available in retail that there is something to suit almost everyone. As with any career choice, it is important to research the area you are interested in thoroughly so that you make an informed decision that will set you on the path to a happy and successful working life.

HANDY HINT

Working in a small independent shop can give you a great introduction to all the tasks involved before you set up your own business. You may gain experience in buying, visual merchandising, promotion, stock control, customer service, finance, and other aspects of working in retail.

Further Information

BOOKS

Andrews, Brad. *The Truth About Retail Jobs: How to Job-Hunt and Career-Change for Retail Jobs.* Emereo, 2009.

Ferguson's Careers in Focus: Retail. Ferguson, 2007.

Field, Shelly. *Career Opportunities in the Retail and Wholesale Industry.* Ferguson, 2009.

O'Malley, Stephanie. *Start Your Retail Career.* Entrepreneur Press, 2008.

Schroeder, Carol L. *Specialty Shop Retailing: Everything You Need to Know to Run Your Own Store.* John Wiley and Sons, 2007.

Stinson, Paul. *Top Careers in Two Years: Retail, Marketing, and Sales.* Ferguson, 2008.

WEB SITES

www.allretailjobs.com
A retail job board listing thousands of job opportunities.

www.bls.gov/oco
For hundreds of different types of jobs—such as those in the retail industry—the Occupational Outlook Handbook gives information on education needed, earnings, job prospects, and more.

www.careeroverview.com/retail-marketing-careers.html
Find information on retail marketing careers, jobs, and training here.

www.nrffoundation.com
The Retail Career Center of the of the National Retail Foundation offers job opportunities, employer partners connections, retail training classes and retail degree programs.

http://retailindustry.about.com
Find research, news, statistics, and career information about the retail industry here.

Glossary

auctioneer a person who announces the items and controls the bidding at an auction (a public sale of property or goods)

barcode a code made up of numbers and lines that can be read by a till at a checkout; it registers the price of goods and helps to record the amount of stock left in the store

bric-a-brac a variety of small objects, usually furniture and other collectable items, sold on the basis that they are unusual or decorative

cooperative an organization owned and run by its workers for their joint benefit

customer traffic the number of people passing through a shop at any one time

deteriorate become gradually worse in quality

human resources also known as "personnel," this refers to the department of a company or organization responsible for hiring and training staff

humidity dampness, or the measure of the amount of moisture in the air

interior design a profession that involves planning the decoration and furnishings inside a house or shop

logistics planning and organizing the movement of goods from one place to another

merchandise goods sold in a store

payroll a list of people employed by a company, with details of how much each person is paid

perishable food that is likely to rot quickly

psychology the scientific study of the human mind and the way in which it works

retail chain a group of stores owned by the same company

statistical describes the use of statistics—data obtained from the study of a large amount of numerical information

stock the supply of goods available for sale in a store

warehouse a large building where goods are stored and from where they are transported to stores for sale, or mailed directly to the customer, in the case of Internet shopping

warranty a written guarantee, given to a person when he or she buys a product, promising to replace or repair it if necessary within a limited period of time

Index